The Ultimate Book of Wisecracks and Insults

Thank you for buying this book. For every copy purchased, we will donate the royalties to Great Ormond Street Hospital Children's Charity in London, England.

The Ultimate Book of Wisecracks and Insults

Sandy Ransford

Robinson Children's Books

Robinson Publishing Ltd
7 Kensington Church Court
London
W8 4SP

First published in the UK by Robinson Children's Books,
an imprint of Robinson Publishing Ltd, 1999

This collection © Robinson Publishing Ltd, 1999
Illustrations © David Mostyn, 1999

Registered Charity No. 235825. © 1989
Great Ormond Street Hospital Children's Charity.

A copy of the British Library Cataloguing in Publication Data for this
title is available from the British Library.

ISBN 1 85487 633 3

Printed and bound in the EC

10 9 8 7 6 5 4 3 2 1

Contents

Introduction

Warning!

"My sister went on a crash diet."
"Is that why she looks a wreck?"

> *"I've got a mechanical mind."*
> *"Yes, but some of your screws are loose."*

"I'll have you know I'm nobody's fool."
"Perhaps you could find someone to adopt you."

> *"Waiter! There's a film on my soup!"*
> *"Then why don't you shut up and watch it?"*

Delivered at the right time and with the right humor, wisecracks and insults are guaranteed to have you – and your friends – falling about laughing. But beware! Making wisecracks is like playing ball. Turn away for a split second and your devastating wisecrack comes right back and hits you on the head. The joke's on you. But when you were wishing you were six feet under, you remember the rules of wisecracks and insults: when someone makes fun of you, get even! And that's when memorizing *The Ultimate Book of Wisecracks and Insults* comes in handy ... So don't hang about, get reading and prepare yourself for lots of fun!

I Never Forget a Face, But . . .

"I never forget a face, but in your case I'll make an exception."

"Don't look out of the window, Lavinia, people will think it's Hallowe'en."

Oh honey, you're a funny 'un –
A face like a pickled onion,
A nose like a squashed tomato,
And teeth like green cheese.

MOLLY: You've got a face like a million dollars.
POLLY: What do you mean?
MOLLY: It's all green and wrinkled.

FIRST MIDDLE-AGED LADY: I've kept my schoolgirl complexion.
SECOND MIDDLE-AGED LADY: Yes, covered in spots.

NEIGHBOR: Haven't I seen you on TV?
ACTOR: Well, I do appear, on and off, you know. How do you like me?
NEIGHBOR: Off.

JEN: Do you think I'll lose my looks as I get older?
KEN: With luck, yes.

MRS WRINKLY: My husband always carries my photograph in his breast pocket. In fact, it once saved his life when a mugger tried to knife him.
MRS CRINKLY: Good heavens! Of course, I'm not surprised, your face would stop anything!

MRS SAGGY: Mrs Wrinkly tried to have a facelift last week.
MRS BAGGY: Tried to?
MRS SAGGY: Yes, they couldn't find a crane strong enough to lift it!

PEGGY: I've just come back from the beauty parlor.
PIGGY: Pity it was closed!

BILL: Gilly has lovely long red hair all down her back.
WILL: Pity it's not on her head!

FAN: I've always admired you. Are your teeth your own?
ACTOR: Whose do you think they are?

4

"Your teeth are like the stars," he said,
As he pressed her hand, so white.
He spoke the truth, for, like the stars,
Her teeth came out at night!

POMPOUS LADY IN ART GALLERY: And I suppose that hideous-looking thing is a modern work of art?
HER COMPANION: Actually, it's a mirror.

"The last time I saw a face like yours I threw it a banana."

JIM: My sister wants to be an actress.
TIM: Is she pretty?
JIM: Well, put it this way, she'd be perfect on radio.

MILES: Our dog's just like one of the family.
GILES: Really? Which one?

MAVE: You remind me of my favorite boxer.
DAVE: Evander Holyfield?
MAVE: No, he's called Fido.

What's the matter with you if your nose runs and your feet smell? You're built upside down!

FATTY: You look as if you've survived a famine – but only just.
THINNY: And you look as if you've caused one.

A very large woman was sitting on a bus next to a man when three senior citizens got on. The bus was crowded and the old folk had to stand. The woman looked at the man and said, "If you were a gentleman you'd get up and let one of these people sit down." "And if you were a lady," he retorted, "you'd get up and let all three of them sit down."

What did the middle-aged lady say as she tucked into her cream buns?
"I'm afraid all this food is going to waist."

Why did the middle-aged lady have to stop eating cream buns?
She was thick to her stomach.

What do sailors say when they see a fat person on a ship?
"A vast behind!"

ANNIE: People keep telling me I'm beautiful.
ANDY: Some people have vivid imaginations.

The rain makes everything beautiful,
The grass and flowers too.
If the rain makes everything beautiful,
Why doesn't it rain on you?

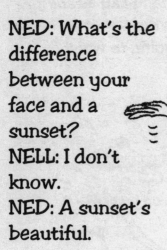

NED: What's the difference between your face and a sunset?
NELL: I don't know.
NED: A sunset's beautiful.

MARIA: This is a genuine Victorian shawl.
MARTIN: Did you make it yourself?

8

MICK: I see you've got your Easter shirt on.

NICK: Why do you call it that?

MICK: Because you've spilt egg all down the front.

Two men were remembering their wedding days. "It was dreadful," said Albert. "I got the most terrible fright." "What happened?" asked Algie. "I married her," replied Albert.

JOHN: Do you feel like a cup of tea?

DON: Oh, yes.

JOHN: You look like one, too – sloppy, hot and wet!

GEMMA: I've been told I look just like an Italian dish.

EMMA: You do.

GEMMA: Really? Sophia Loren? Gina Lollobrigida?

EMMA: No, spaghetti bolognese.

9

ROMEO: You remind me of a film star.
JULIET: Which one?
ROMEO: Lassie.

GILL: Your sister uses too much make-up.
JEN: Do you think so?
GILL: Yes. It's so thick that if you tell her
a joke five minutes after she's
stopped laughing her face is still
smiling!

SIMON: I was going to buy you a handkerchief for
your birthday.
SARAH: That was a kind thought. Why didn't you?
SIMON: I couldn't find one big enough for your nose.

SON: The guys all say I look like a werewolf.
MOTHER: Shut up and comb your face.

MRS TIDDLES: Do you like my dress? I bought it for a very low price.

MRS TOODLES: You mean for a ridiculous figure.

OTTO: Is your girlfriend pretty or ugly?

OLLIE: I'd say she was pretty ugly.

FATHER: You eat like a pig, Edward. Do you know what a pig is?

EDWARD: Yes, a hog's son.

"Is that your face or are you wearing your hair back to front today?"

11

ATTENDANT IN THE CHAMBER OF HORRORS: Could you keep moving on, please, madam, we're stock-taking today.

BELINDA: James told me last night that he'd met the most beautiful girl in the world.
BARBARA: Oh, I'm so sorry. I thought he was going to marry you.

Why did Frankenstein's monster give up boxing? In case he spoiled his looks.

Two old friends met, ten years after the end of the Second World War. One said, "Is that your face or are you still wearing your gas mask?"

WIFE TO HUSBAND: I'll have you know I've got the face of a teenager!
HUSBAND TO WIFE: Then you should give it back, you're wearing it out.

PATIENT: The trouble is, Doctor, I keep pulling ugly faces.
DOCTOR: Don't worry, I don't expect anyone will notice.

"I wouldn't say Bertie has big ears but he's often mistaken for Mr Spock."

Knock, knock.
Who's there?
Alec.
Alec who?
Alec most people but I don't like your face.

Knock, knock.
Who's there?
Fred.
Fred who?
Fred I can't stand the sight of yours!

Knock, knock.
Who's there?
Olga.
Olga who?
Olga home if
you're horrid
to me again.

Knock, knock.
Who's there?
Hali.
Hali who?
Halitosis – your
breath smells
awful!

Knock, knock.
Who's there?
Hawaii.
Hawaii who?
I was fine until you
turned up!

14

CHERRY: What's Cheryl like?
JERRY: She's a slick chick.
CHERRY: You mean she's like a greasy chicken?

"My mother-in-law's so ugly she can make her own yoghurt by staring at a pint of milk."

DARREN: I'm so tired I feel like an old sock.
SHARON: I thought there was a funny smell in here!

BILL: What would it take to make you give me a kiss?
GILL: An anaesthetic.

TEDDIE: What's that terribly
ugly thing on your
shoulders?
NEDDIE: Help! What is it?
TEDDIE: Your head!

HARRY: I've a soft spot for you.
MARY: Really?
HARRY: Yes, in the middle of a bog!

AMY: That awful woman down the road said Dad
wasn't fit to live with pigs!
MOTHER: What did you say?
AMY: Oh, I defended him, I said of course he was!

SID: All the boys
at school call me
Big Head.
MOTHER:
Never mind,
just pop
down to the
store for me
and collect the
five pounds of
potatoes I
ordered in your
cap.

MAISIE: Where were you born?
DAISY: In the local hospital.
MAISIE: I always thought there was something wrong with you!

ROMEO: Your cheeks are like petals.
JULIET: Really?
ROMEO: Yes, bicycle pedals.

JAMES: I call my girlfriend Peach.
JOHN: Because she's beautiful?
JAMES: No, because she's got a heart of stone!

JONAH: Did you hear about Jim Jenkins's wife?
MONA: No, what about her?
JONAH: She's so ugly that when they got married everyone kissed *him*.

Brainbox

JOHN: How do you keep a thicko in suspense?
JIM: I don't know.
JOHN: Tell you next week.

How do you make a thicko laugh on Friday?
Tell him a joke on Monday.

LARRY: I've changed my mind.
BARRY: Thank goodness! Does the new one work any better?

Did you hear about the boy who was so stupid that when he picked his nose he tore the lining out of his cap?

IAN: How dare you tell everyone I'm a fool!
IRIS: Sorry, I didn't know it was a secret.

How can you kill an idiot with a coin?
Throw it under a bus.

HILDA: I love biscuits!
TILDA: That's because you're crackers!

What's
bright red
and really
stupid?
A blood clot.

BRIAN: How long can someone live without a brain?
RYAN: How old are you?

"I see you've burnt your ear. Were you doing the ironing when the phone rang?"

Why did the other idiot burn his ear?
He was listening to the match.

Why did the idiot plant pennies in his garden?
He wanted to raise some hard cash.

LYN: I don't like soup.
BRYN: I expect you can't get it to stay on the fork.

What did the biscuits say to the almonds? "You're nuts and we're crackers!"

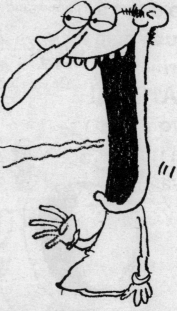

NEIL: What's the difference between Nellie and a boring TV program?
NOEL: You can turn off a boring TV program!

TRIXIE: When I die I'm going to leave my brain to science.
TRACEY: I suppose every little helps.

22

"He's so thick that after he'd watched a gardening program on TV he started watering the light bulbs."

SON: I want to drive a bus when I grow up.
FATHER: I won't stand in your way.

How did the researcher take a census of people in the dumbo's class?
He used an ape-recorder.

MICK: Tim's gone to live in the city.
NICK: Why's that?
MICK: He'd read in the papers that the country was at war.

MAN IN CLOTHES STORE: I'd like a blue shirt to match my eyes, please.
STOREKEEPER: I'm sorry, sir, we don't have any blue shirts. But we do have some soft hats that would match your head.

Did you hear about the boy who was known as Fog?
He was thick and wet.

JEN: You look as if you'd find it hard to chew gum and walk at the same time.
KEN: And you look as if you'd find it hard to chew gum and breathe at the same time!

BARRY: You're like uncultivated woodland.
GARY: Really?
BARRY: Yes, totally dense.

JANE: Do you ever do any gardening?
WAYNE: Not often. Why?
JANE: You look as if you could do with some remedial weeding.

Knock, knock.
Who's there?
G.I.
G.I. who?
G.I. don't know who I am!

HOLLY: Do you ever find life boring?
DOLLY: I didn't until I met you.

He's so stupid he thinks Camelot is where Arabs park their camels.

25

She's so stupid she thinks
hair spray is something
you use to get rid of
rabbits.

He's so stupid he thinks a
cucumber is something
you play pool with.

Chris is so stupid he thinks
Christmas Eve is a tug of war.

He's so stupid he thinks double-glazing means a man
wearing glasses who's had too much to drink.

She's so stupid she thinks a shoplifter is a very strong person who goes round picking up shops.

CROSSWORD FAN: I've been trying to think of a word for two weeks!
FRIEND: How about a fortnight?

PATIENT: What does the X-ray of my brain show?
DOCTOR: Nothing.

What happened when Dumbo went to a mind-reader?
They gave him his money back.

27

JAKE: That ointment the vet gave me for the dog makes my fingers smart.
BLAKE: Why don't you rub some on your head, then?

AVRIL: Sometimes I really like you.
APRIL: When's that?
AVRIL: When you're not yourself.

CHARLIE: Do you think I'm intelligent?
CHRISSIE: I'd like to say "yes" but I've been brought up to tell the truth.

EMMA: I'd like to say something nice about you as it's your birthday.
GEMMA: Why don't you?
EMMA: Because I can't think of a single thing to say!

IVAN: They say Ian has a dual personality.
IVOR: Let's hope the other one is brighter than this one!

MADGE: Your body's quite well organized.
MARTIN: How do you mean?
MADGE: The weakest part – your brain – is protected by the strongest – your thick skull!

What did the builder say when he saw his none-too-bright assistant laying the lawn at a new house? "Green side up!"

NELLIE: I have an open mind.
KELLY: Yes, there's nothing in it.

REG: I keep talking to myself.
ROGER: I'm not surprised – no one else would listen to you!

ZOE: I'm sure I'm right.
CHLOE: You're as right as rain – all wet!

"I wouldn't say he's thick-headed – but he's the only person I know who's allowed to ride a motorbike without a helmet."

JOE: What does "opaque" mean?
JOSE: Something light can't pass through – like your head!

30

MARIE: Two heads are better than one.
GARY: In your case none might be better than one!

DARREN: What will Clive do when he leaves school? I can't see him being bright enough to get a job.
SANDRA: He could always be a ventriloquist's dummy.

HAZEL: I wonder what my IQ is?
HEATHER: Don't worry about it, it's nothing.

"He's got a chip on his shoulder."
"It's probably from the block of wood above."

"I always like to think the best of people, that's why I think of you as a complete idiot."

"She has great depth, you know."
"Yes, depth of ignorance."

"She has a mind of her own."
"Of course she does. No one else would want it."

"Did you hear someone has invented a coffin that just covers the head? It's for people like you who're dead from the neck up!"

BERTIE: You remind me of a Greek statue.
GERTIE: Do you mean you think I'm beautiful?
BERTIE: Yes, beautiful, but not all there.

ROY: They say ignorance is bliss.
RITA: Then you should be the happiest boy in the world.

BENNIE: I've been told I must lose ten pounds of surplus fat.
KENNY: You could always cut off your head.

CARY: There's no point in telling you a joke with a double meaning.
MARY: Why not?
CARY: You wouldn't get either of them.

33

"I'd like you to accept my opinion for what it's worth."
"That means you owe me a cent."

BILL: I never act stupid.
HIL: No, with you it's the real thing.

"You're only as old as you act."
"That means you must be about three."

"You can read his mind in his face."
"Yes, it's usually a complete blank."

"I've been thinking hard about what you said."
"You mean it's hard for you to think."

"My brother said he'd tell me everything he knows."
"He must have been speechless."

STELLA: Tracey has a ready wit.
SHEILA: Perhaps she could let us know when it's about to start!

DANIEL: Being clever isn't everything.
DENZIL: In your case it isn't anything.

"My sister's going out with David."
"Any girl who goes out with David must be able to appreciate the simpler things in life."

"They say Margaret is a raving beauty."
"You mean she's escaped from a loony bin?"

"In one way Julian is lucky. If he went out of his mind no one would notice the difference."

"I feel sorry for your little mind – all alone in that great big head."

"Jonathan ought to be a boxer. Someone might knock him conscious."

"Why is your brother always flying off the handle?"
"Because he's got a screw loose."

"His speech started at 2 p.m. sharp."
"And finished at 3 p.m. dull."

"They call him Baby-face."
"Does that mean he's got a brain to match?"

"Don't let your mind wander. It's not strong enough to be allowed out on its own."

"Does she have something on her mind?"
"Only if she's wearing a hat."

FIRST EXPLORER: There's one thing about Jenkinson.
SECOND EXPLORER: What's that?
FIRST EXPLORER: He could go to headhunters' country without any fear – they'd have no interest in him.

BRIAN: Let's play a game of wits.
DIANE: No, let's play something you can play too.

Cracking Lines

JOANNE: How many people work in your college?
JOHAN: About half of them.

FATHER: Alan! You mustn't fight! You must learn to give and take! ALAN: But I did! I gave him a black eye and took his football!

ANDREW: I'm too tired to mow the lawn.
FATHER: Listen, son, hard work never killed anyone.
ANDREW: And I don't want to be the first!

PASSENGER: Will this bus take me into town?
DRIVER: Which part?
PASSENGER: All of me, of course!

JANE: Do you like me?
WAYNE: As girls go, you're fine. And the sooner you go the better!

HARRY: Every time I walk past a girl she sighs.
WILLIAM: Yes – with relief!

FREDA: Boys whisper they love me.
FRED: Well, they wouldn't admit it out loud, would they?

LAURA: Whenever I go to the corner store, the storekeeper shakes my hand.
LIONEL: I expect it's to make sure you don't put it in his till.

JERRY: Is that a new perfume I smell?
KERRY: It is, and you do!

FENTON: You'll just have to give me credit.
BENTON: Well, I'm certainly not giving you cash!

DYLAN: I take lots of exercise.
DUNCAN: I thought so. That's why you're so long-winded.

BERNIE: Why have you given me this piece of rope?
ERNIE: They say if you give someone enough rope they'll hang themselves!

PETER: My brother wants to work badly.
ANITA: As I remember, he usually does.

MICHAEL: It's hard for my sister to eat.
MAUREEN: Why?
MICHAEL: She can't bear to stop talking.

BOSS: Are you willing to do an honest day's work?
SECRETARY: Yes, as long as you give me an honest week's pay for it.

GORDON: My wallet's full of big bills.
GRAHAM: All unpaid, I expect.

SON: How old are you, Dad?
DAD: Oh, around 35.
SON: I expect you've been around it a few times!

SON: Dad kept asking for glasses of water
when he was in hospital.
DAUGHTER: I expect that's how they knew
he was going out of his mind.

"He reminds me of a bowl of custard."
"Yes, yellow and thick."

"They say he works eight hours and sleeps
eight hours. Problem is, they're the same
eight hours."

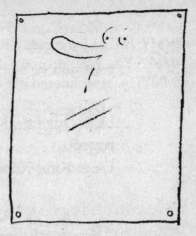

"When my dad finally passed his fourth-grade spelling test he was so excited he cut himself shaving."

"My dad once stopped a man ill-treating a donkey. It was a case of brotherly love."

"My brother's looking for a wife. Trouble is, he can't find a woman who loves him as much as he loves himself."

"Your sister's boyfriend certainly has staying power. In fact, he never leaves."

JIMMY: Is that lemonade OK?
TIMMY: Yes. Why do you ask?
JIMMY: I just wondered if it was as sour as your face.

LEE: Our family's descended from royalty.
DEE: King Kong?

ANNE: Do you think I look awful in this dress?
DAN: You could look worse – if I had better eyesight!

MARY: Do you think my sister's pretty?
GARY: Well, let's just say if you pulled her pigtail she'd probably say "oink, oink!"

CHERYL: They say I have an infectious laugh.
MERYL: In that case don't laugh near me!

JAN: My little brother is a real pain.
NAN: Things could be worse.
JAN: How?
NAN: He could be twins.

"Do you like my new baby sister? The stork brought her."
"Hmm, it looks as if the stork dropped her on her head."

"My sister went on a crash diet."
"Is that why she looks a wreck?"

"My brother's on a seafood diet."
"Really?"
"Yes, the more he sees food the more he eats."

"My mother gets migraine."
"Probably because her halo's too tight."

PENNY: No one could call your dad a quitter.
KENNY: No, he's been sacked from every job he's ever had.

WINNIE: I was cut out to be a genius.
GINNY: Pity no one put the pieces together properly.

TERRY: When my mother was young she had a coming-out party.
GERRY: When they saw her they probably sent her back in again.

"I hear she was a war baby."
"I'm not surprised – I expect her parents took one look at her and started fighting."

"He has a heart of gold."
"And teeth to match."

"Does your brother keep himself clean?"
"Oh, yes. He takes a bath every month whether he needs one or not."

"His left eye must be fascinating."
"Why do you say that?"
"Because his right eye looks at it all the time."

"How can she be so fat? She eats like a bird!"
"Yes, a vulture!"

"She once had a million-dollar figure. Trouble is, inflation set in."

"They say he has a leaning towards blondes."
"Yes, but they keep pushing him back."

"My boyfriend only has two faults – everything he says and everything he does!"

"He thinks everyone worships the ground he crawled out of."

"I hear she doesn't care for a man's company."
"Not unless he owns it."

"They say he's a very careful person."
"Well, he likes to economize on soap and water."

"A friend in need is – someone to avoid!"

"That girl looks like Helen Black."
"She looks even worse in white."

RICH LADY: That painting you did of me doesn't do me justice.
ARTIST: Madam, it's not justice you want, it's mercy!

NEW WIFE: Will you love me when I'm old and fat and ugly?
NEW HUSBAND: Of course I do!

"Bill and Gill make a perfect pair, don't they?"
"They certainly do. She's a pill and he's a headache."

"He will never be a leader of men."
"No, but he's a great follower of women!"

"Doesn't he look distinguished?"
"He'd look better if he were extinguished."

"I hear he has a quick mind."
"Yes, he's a real scheme engine."

The best way of saving money is to forget who you borrowed it from.

OWEN: Thank you so much for lending me that money. I shall be everlastingly in your debt.
LENNY: That's what I'm afraid of!

What's a definition of gossip?
Ear pollution.

RONNIE: I can trace my family tree way back.
BONNIE: Yes, back to the time you lived in it!

"She's so ugly that when a wasp stings her it shuts its eyes."

"They say her tongue's so sharp she can slice bread with it."

LAURIE: We should all do our bit to clean up the environment.
MOTHER: I agree. You could start with your room.

What's another name for pollution? The effluence of affluence.

"They say cleanliness is next to godliness."
"With some people it's next to impossible!"

"Does he tell lies?"
"Let's just say his memory exaggerates."

JANE: I'll cook dinner. What would you like?
SHANE: Good life insurance.

56

"I got a gold watch for my girlfriend."
"I wish I could make a trade like that!"

"They say he's going places."
"The sooner the better!"

"Harry's very good for other people's health. Whenever they see him coming they go for a long walk!"

"Did you say he told good gags?"
"No, I said he needed one!"

"Did you say he had a big mouth?"
"Put it this way, he's the only person I
know who can eat a banana
sideways!"

"When it comes to helping
others, she'll stop at
nothing!"

"I always think twice
before speaking."
"I expect it gives you time
to think up something
really nasty."

"She has real
polish."
"Only on her
shoes."

"She has an answer to every problem."
"Yes, but they're always wrong."

"I hear she's highly strung."
"She should be!"

"He bought her engagement ring from a famous millionaire."
"Who? The owner of Price Check?"

"She's got so fat she can sit around a table all by herself."

"He's watching his weight."
"Yes, watching it go up!"

"He's a light eater."
"Yes, as soon as it's light he starts
eating!"

"Does he have big ears?"
"Let's just say he's very good at swatting
flies."

Two
Left
Feet

NOVICE TENNIS PLAYER: How would you have played that last shot?
COACH: In disguise!

MAY: What position does your brother play in the school football team?
JAY: I think he's one of the drawbacks.

DICKIE: I hear the team's prospects are looking up.
NICKY: Oh good, are you leaving it then?

Bob had just missed a shot at goal, which meant the other team won. "I could kick myself," he groaned, as the players came off the field.

"Don't bother," said the captain, "you'd miss."

COACH: Why did you miss that shot?
PLAYER: I sprained my ankle.
COACH: That's a lame excuse.

CAPTAIN: Why didn't you stop the ball?
PLAYER: I thought that was what the net was for.

MAUREEN: I hear Mattie likes hockey. DOREEN: That's because she's such a bully!

FIRST TRAMPOLINIST: How's life?
SECOND TRAMPOLINIST: Oh, up and down, you know.

WILL: Why do you call that new player Cinderella?
BILL: Because he's always running away from the ball.

Young Horace was being taught how to box, but so far hadn't landed a single blow on his opponent. "Don't worry, lad," said his teacher, "keep swinging, the draft might give him a cold."

"Why do you call Susie a lobster?"
"Because she's such a lousy tennis player."

What did young Teddy say when Neddy shot towards him in the archery class?
"That was an arrow escape."

Why can't horses dance?
Because they've got two left feet.

"Why do you call Robert a baby swimmer? He's ten years old." "Because he can only crawl."

Knock, knock.
Who's there?
Victor.
Victor who?
Victor his tennis shorts.

Why was the boxer known as Picasso?
Because he spent most of his time on the canvas.

Paul broke a rib playing football. The following week the doctor asked him how he was feeling. "I keep getting a stitch in my side," said Paul.

"Good," said the doctor. "That shows the bones are knitting."

The home team lost and young David came off the pitch looking very unhappy. "I've never played so badly before," he groaned.

"Oh, you've played before, have you?" said the captain.

YOUNG FOOTBALLER: How do I stand for a team trial?
SELECTOR: You don't stand, you grovel.

The baseball match was very dull. "I'm surprised the crowd doesn't shout at them," said one of the spectators.

"Difficult to shout when you're asleep," said his neighbor.

GOLFER: My doctor says I must give up golf.
HIS FRIEND: He's seen you play, too, has he?

ANOTHER GOLFER: I love golf. I could play like this for ever.
HIS PARTNER: Don't you ever want to improve?

ERIC: Did you hear that United play the National Anthem before every match?
DEREK: Really? Are they *that* patriotic?
ERIC: No, it's to make sure everyone in the team can stand up.

BEN: You'd be a great player if it weren't for two things.
LEN: What are they?
BEN: Your feet.

"There's only one way we can raise the level of our team's performance."
"What's that?"
"Play on the top of a mountain."

At a football match between two neighborhood teams a man asked the price of admission. "Twenty dollars, sir," was the reply.

"Here's ten," said the man. "There's only one team worth watching."

What was the star player awarded when he missed a penalty?
A constellation prize.

FREDDIE: How's the new player coming along?
TEDDY: He's trying.
FREDDIE: I've heard he's very trying.

"There's always a long queue when our team play – queuing to get out!"

"Why do you call him a wonder player?"
"Because when I watch him I wonder if he's ever played before!"

Knock, knock.
Who's there?
Thermos.
Thermos who?
Thermos be a better player than you!

Knock, knock.
Who's there?
Dozen.
Dozen who?
Dozen anyone know how to play?

Knock, knock.
Who's there?
N.E.
N.E. who?
N.E. body could play
better than you!

Knock, knock.
Who's there?
Anatole.
Anatole who?
Anatole me you were
hopeless.

A fan approached a famous tennis player. "May I have your autograph, please?" she asked.

The tennis player was in a hurry, so he said, "I don't really play tennis, you know."

"I'm aware of that," said the fan. "But I'd like your autograph anyway."

It was raining, and the goalkeeper had let in several goals. As he came off the field he sniffed, and said, "I think I've caught a cold."

"I'm pleased to hear you can catch something," replied a fellow player.

BIG-HEADED PLAYER: I've been told I have music in my feet.
HIS FRIEND: Yes, two flats!

VETERAN PLAYER: How old are you?
SECOND VETERAN PLAYER: Thirty-five. But I don't look it, do I?
FIRST VETERAN PLAYER: No, but you used to.

It was a warm day and the baseball player kept missing his shots. After the game he sighed and said, "What couldn't I do with a long, cold drink."

"Hit it?" enquired a fellow player.

What happened when the umpire had a brain transplant?
The brain rejected him

"I've never refereed a football match before. Do I have to run after the ball?"

"No, after the match."

The referee failed to turn up at a local match, so the captain asked for a volunteer. One man stepped forward.

"You *have* refereed a match before?" asked the captain.

"Yes," replied the man. "And if you don't believe me, ask my three friends up in the stand."

"In that case," said the captain, "I'm afraid we can't use you."

"Why not?" asked the man.

"Because no one who's ever refereed a match *has* three friends."

"That player's out of this world!"
"The captain often wishes he were!"

One player played a terrible match, missing all his shots. So in the days before the next game he trained and practiced very hard, and was quite pleased with the result. "Notice any difference?" he asked the captain.

The captain studied him for a moment. "You've shaved off your mustache," he replied.

What's the difference between a goalkeeper who's asleep and one who's awake?
With some goalkeepers it's not easy to tell!

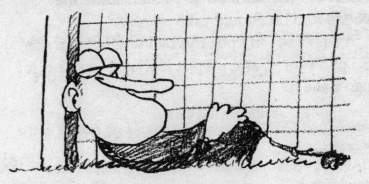

Young Andy took an afternoon off school to go to a football match. He said he was going to his grandfather's funeral. Unfortunately for Andy one of the teachers was at the game, where the local team lost 6 – 0, and recognized him.

"So this is your grandfather's funeral, is it?" asked the teacher.

"Seems to be," said Andy. "That's him in goal."

PLAYER: I might play better if I didn't get such poultry wages.
MANAGER: You mean "paltry."
PLAYER: No I don't, I mean "poultry," it's chickenfeed.

A very bad golfer once hit a ball on to an ant hill, but when he tried to hit if off again he kept missing the ball and hitting the ant hill, killing many of the ants. Eventually only two ants remained. "I suppose," said one to the other, "that if we want to stay alive we'd better climb on to the ball."

What did the fat man say when someone suggested he should take up golf?

"It's no use – if I put the ball where I can see it I can't hit it, and if I put it where I can hit it I can't see it."

ANGRY GOLFER: You must be the worst caddie in the world!
CADDIE: I doubt it, that would be too much of a coincidence!

DESPONDENT GOLFER: I'd move heaven and earth to get a better score.
CADDIE: Concentrate on heaven, you've already moved enough earth!

What did they call the crazy golfer? A crack putt!

GOLFER: Have you packed all my golf gear in the car?
WIFE: Yes, dear; clubs, map, compass, emergency rations ...

GOLFER: Do you like my game?
PARTNER: Not bad, but I prefer golf.

UMPIRE: Out!
PLAYER: What for?
UMPIRE: The rest of the match!

Why didn't the idiot go water-skiing when he was on holiday? He couldn't find a sloping lake.

Why didn't the idiot play water-polo when he was on holiday?
He couldn't get the horse into the water.

"Your cheeks are like peaches – football peetches."

Did you hear about the boy who ran away with a football club? The police made him bring it back.

What goes in pink and comes out blue?
A swimmer in winter.

What's yellow and has 22 legs?
Banana United.

Did you hear about the two
fat boys who ran in a race?
One ran in short bursts; the other in
burst shorts.

OLD GOLFER: How did you get on in your first game?
NEW GOLFER: I took 65 strokes.
OLD GOLFER: That's pretty good.
NEW GOLFER: Yes, and next week I'm going to try the
second hole.

NOBBY: I got sacked from the team
last week.
BOBBY: What for?
NOBBY: For good.

Knock, knock.
Who's there?
Stopwatch.
Stopwatch who?
Stopwatch you're
doing this minute!

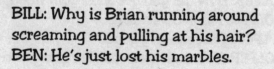

BILL: Why is Brian running around
screaming and pulling at his hair?
BEN: He's just lost his marbles.

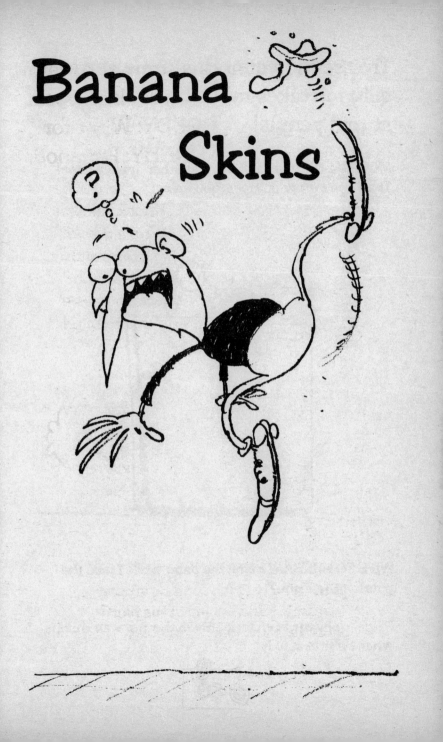

This section contains some very silly mistakes made by some very stupid people!

MOTHER: No, you can't have another apple, Simon! They don't grow on trees, you know!

WIFE TO HUSBAND: Boil the baby while I feed the potatoes, will you?

"Nigel's always been lucky. Even the sun was shining when he first saw it."

MOTHER: Remember, Samantha, a young lady never crumbles her bread or rolls in her soup.

NOTICE ON THE WINDOW OF A BAKER'S SHOP: Vienna rolls.
SCRAWLED UNDERNEATH:
London swings.

"My grandfather is retarded on a pension."

"Her foot slipped and she bruised herself quite badly in the pantry."

A man ran after a lady in the street, tapped her on the shoulder and said, "Hello, darling."

"Do I know you?" she asked coldly.

The man was covered in confusion. "Oh, please excuse me," he said. "I thought you were my wife. You look just like her behind."

"In a word, I don't think that's right."

"Nothing that politician says is worth the paper it's written on."

SPEAKER AT MEETING: . . . and his words will be forever printed on my mind. Let me read them to you.

FATHER: George! Don't let the dog hang his head out of the window while driving!

"On holiday I chased a dog on a bicycle but I couldn't catch it."

FROM A NEWSPAPER: Pieces of the giant cake were delivered to 200 senior citizens living locally in Mr Jones's van.

ANNE: Did you read the book I lent you?
ANDREW: Well, I read part of it all the way through.

BOSS: What were you doing going outside and sitting on your tea-break?

MOTHER: If you don't come back, I shan't let you go again.

LECTURER: This happens a hundred times out of a hundred – in other words, almost always.

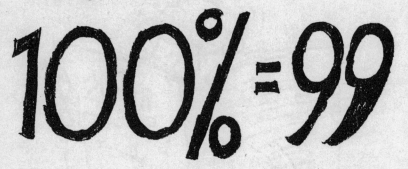

SECRETARY: Last year I had to communicate to the city every day.

NOTICE BY A VILLAGE POND:
Beware! All of this ice is frozen.

NOTICE BY A RIVER: When this sign is under water the towpath is flooded.

FROM A NEWSPAPER: Because the elderly find it difficult to climb the hill the council have agreed to put a seat at the top.

FROM A SCHOOL TEST-PAPER: Tadpoles eat one another until they become frogs.

85

FROM ANOTHER SCHOOL PAPER: Blood is made up of red and white corkscrews.

BILLY: Is your cold better?
TILLY: I've got a very bad head but I hope to shake it off soon.

MRS GREEN: How's your new house?
MRS BROWN: The roof needs mending. In last week's storm rain was coming down the walls like water.

TEACHER: Don't speak when you're talking to me!

FARMER BROWN: Without a word of warning all the sheep ran across the road.

POLICE SPOKESMAN: There have been a number of fatalities on that road, but no serious accidents.

"The wives of American Indians were called squaws, and their children were called squawkers."

"After Mrs Green bought a cow she supplied us all with milk, cream and eggs."

HEAD TEACHER: We have been trying to do away with school uniforms. We hope to end up with the boys wearing just a tie and the girls a skirt.

FROM A NEWSPAPER: After the explosion six people were taken to hospital suffering from mild buns.

NOTICE: The school choir's annual picnic will be hell on the village green.

DESCRIPTION OF A WEDDING DRESS: The skirt was long and gathered, and fell to her ankles.

FROM A RADIO REPORT: The drugs were discovered by a sniffer dog hidden in a drink can.

HORRIFIED FATHER: If my mother were alive she'd turn in her grave!

FROM AN ESSAY: In France even the pheasants used to drink wine.

89

MRS WHITE: I think the dog must have fleas, as he keeps on etching.

HISTORY STUDENT: The king knighted him with his royal specter.

ENGLISH STUDENT: Poetry is where every line begins with a capital letter.

"A man who makes spectacles is called an optimist."

"Insects is burnt in church services."

"Venison is a city in northern Italy with lots of canals."

"If gravity didn't exist we would all fly away."

"Nuclear weapons are made from geraniums."

FROM A CHURCH NOTICEBOARD: Will anyone who has relatives buried in the churchyard please keep them in order.

FOR SALE: Antique porcelain vase, property of elderly lady only slightly cracked.

WANTED: Male waitress.

FOR SALE: Semi-detached horse overlooking seafront.

WANTED: Woman wants cleaning two days a week.

ADVERTISEMENT: Make your raincoat really repellent with our plasticizing spray.

MOTHER: I do wish you'd listen to me when you're speaking, Dennis!

NOTICE IN A RESTAURANT: For those customers who have small children and don't know it there is a playground outside.

"If we want to keep our heads above water we must keep our ears to the ground."

"Since I got bitten by mosquitoes I've been suffering from irrigation."

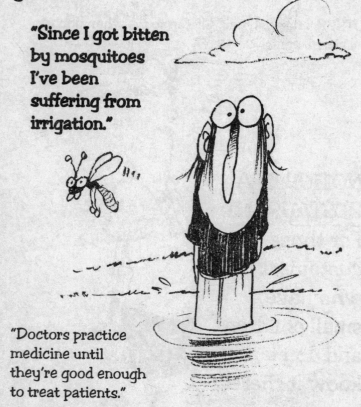

"Doctors practice medicine until they're good enough to treat patients."

"Margarine is a fat made from imitation cows."

"A centurion was a Roman soldier who was a hundred years old."

"A lady vicar is called a vixen."

"Moths eat holes in your clothes."

"Socrates died from an overdose of wedlock."

DID YOU HEAR ABOUT THE DUMBO:

... who thought that "bacteria" meant the back door of a café?

... who thought that an earwig was something to keep your ears warm?

... who thought that "eureka!" meant that you don't smell too good?

96

... who thought that "Urdu"
was something you got at a
hairdresser's?

... who thought that graffiti was a kind of
Italian food?

... who thought that a prawn was a
chesspiece?

... who thought that "massacre"
meant a kind of eye make-up?

LOONY SHOPPING LIST

1 tin of tartan paint
1 pint of gravy
a bottle of invisible ink
6 hard-boiled sheep's eggs
a left-handed pencil
a hot ice cream
music for a rubber band

If you want to make someone feel a complete fool ask them to read the following and then repeat it quickly:
O WATER NAS IAM.

JENNY: I've heard they're not going to grow bananas in Jamaica any longer.
KENNY: Why not?
JENNY: They're long enough already!

A man was poised on a diving board high above a swimming pool when a voice cried out, "Don't dive, there's no water in the pool!"

"That's all right," the man yelled back, "I can't swim."

LOCAL: Are you lost?
STRANGER: No, I'm here. It's the bus station that's lost.

NOTICE IN STORE WINDOW:
Boots and shoes polished inside.

NOTICE IN HAIRDRESSER'S: Hair cut while you wait.

LETTER FROM A TRAVEL AGENT: The flight you requested is fully booked but if someone falls out we'll let you know.

NOTICE ON A SEASIDE PIER:
Don't throw
People below

NOTICE AT A RAIL STATION: These toilets are out of order. Please use platform 6.

NOTICE IN A RESTAURANT WINDOW: Eat in the Cosy Café, where good food is an unexpected pleasure.

NOTICE IN A LAUNDERETTE: Leave all your clothes here, ladies, and spend the afternoon shopping.

NOTICE IN A STORE WINDOW: Visit our bargain basement on the sixth floor.

NOTICE IN AN OFFICE TEAROOM: Will staff please empty the teapots and stand upside down on the draining board.

NOTICE IN A STORE: Customers giving orders will be executed promptly.

NOTICE IN A PARK: No person may walk, lie, play ball games or exercise dogs on the grass in this pleasure ground.

The Joke's On Me

TERRY: I spend hours in front of the mirror admiring my looks. Do you think that's vanity?
JERRY: No, just a vivid imagination.

OLDER BROTHER: When I was a sailor I sailed both ways across the Atlantic without taking a bath.
YOUNGER BROTHER: I always said you were a dirty double crosser!

SINGER: Did you notice how my voice filled the hall?
MANAGER: Yes. And did you notice how many people left to make room for it?

SALLY: I can play the piano by ear.
WALLY: And I can fiddle with my toes!

103

Did you hear about the flower arranger's children?
One was a budding genius, the other was a blooming
idiot!

MAGGIE: Are you
superstitious?
AGGIE: No.
MAGGIE: In that
case please lend
me thirteen
dollars.

NELLIE: Do you believe in free speech?
KELLY: Of course.
NELLIE: In that case may I use your phone?

GILES: Can you lend me a quarter? I want to phone a
friend.
MILES: Here's fifty cents. Phone them all.

JIM: How do you find my breath?
TIM: Offensive. It's keeping you alive!

BILL: Ben's good at everything he does.
WILL: And as far as I can see he usually does nothing!

GLORIA: Boys fall in love with me at first sight.
GORDON: I bet they change their minds when they take a second look!

ESKIMO GIRL: There's something I'd like to give you.
ESKIMO BOY: What?
ESKIMO GIRL: The cold shoulder.

HAROLD: We should all try to fight air pollution.
HENRY: You could start by stopping breathing.

COMEDIAN: Do you find me entertaining?
FRIEND: I'd say you were too dumb to entertain a thought.

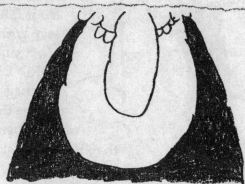

DAVE: He'd never hurt a fly.
MAVE: No, he'd rather hurt people.

BOSS: It would take ten men to fill my shoes.
SECRETARY (ASIDE): And it took ten cows to make them.

BRIAN: Shall I put the TV on?
RYAN: It might look better than that shirt you're wearing.

SAMANTHA: Don't I look gorgeous today?
SUSANNAH: It's a treat for people to see you. After all, they have to pay to get into a freak show.

WIFE: Did you like the food I cooked for you?
HUSBAND: Let's just say it was a real swill dinner.

BARNEY: My girlfriend's cooking's like a good man.
ARNIE: What do you mean?
BARNEY: It's hard to keep down!

PETER: Her cooking gives food for thought.
PAUL: It certainly doesn't give food for eating!

JAMES: The thing about John is that he believes in the conservation of energy.
JORDAN: Yes, he conserves all the energy he can.

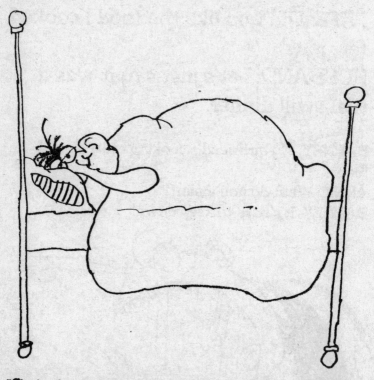

"She's always talking with her mouth full – of words!"

"He's not really an upright character. In fact, even his shadow is crooked."

SISTER: I never wear lipstick.
BROTHER: No, because you can't keep your mouth still for long enough to put it on!

WIFE: Did you really marry me because you'd heard my uncle had left me a fortune?
HUSBAND: No, I'd have married you no matter who had left you a fortune.

NEIGHBOR 1: How old do you think I am?
NEIGHBOR 2: I don't know, but I've heard your grandfather was called Adam.

SECRETARY: I work for you and I admire you.
BOSS: Of course you do. If you didn't you'd be sacked.

SUSIE: Is it true that your dad is a miracle worker?
SALLY: Yes. It's a miracle when he works.

"They say the only exercise he gets is watching horror films on TV."
"How does that give him exercise?"
"They make his flesh creep."

"Don't you think my dress is becoming?"
"Yes, becoming worn out."

"His clothes never go out of style – they look just as old-fashioned every year."

"What are little white things in your head that bite?"
"Teeth!"

TEACHER: I think I shall call you "Corn."
SAMMY: Why?
TEACHER: Because you're always at the foot of the class.

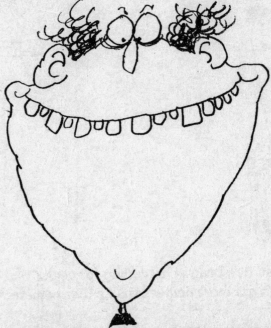

JENNIFER: I want to be the toast of the town.
JONATHAN: Is that why you lie in the sun all day?

"He's so stupid he probably couldn't spell 'Anna' backwards."

"He can't see further than the nose on his face."
"No, but with *his* nose that's quite a distance."

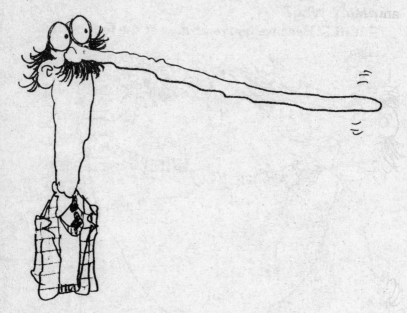

"They say he's been at university for years."
"Yes, he's got more degrees than a thermometer."

"My wife is very dear to me."
"Yes, I believe she costs you a fortune."

"My husband's a millionaire."
"He was a multi-millionaire before you married him."

"They say his parents are real swingers."
"From tree to tree?"

NORMAN: Nigel plays the mouth organ. He's had many requests.
NORMA: So I've heard. But he keeps on playing anyway.

DINER: Will the band play requests?
WAITER: Yes, sir. What would you like?
DINER: I'd like them to play cards.

"They say music has a terrible effect on him. It makes him play his violin."

"Joey said I was as pretty as a flower."
"Would that be a cauliflower?"

"He asked me to tell him everything I know."
"I bet you were speechless."

"They say she's a woman of breeding."
"Yes, I heard she has a lot of children."

"Words fail me."
"I've noticed you don't know how to use them."

"I like nightlife."
"Owls, mice, bats . . . ?"

"I've been told I have beautiful
blue eyes."
"How would you like to have
black ones?"

"My sister's never
said an unkind thing
about anyone."
"No, because she
never talks about
anyone but herself."

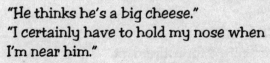

"He thinks he's a big cheese."
"I certainly have to hold my nose when
I'm near him."

"He thinks he's a big gun."
"He should be careful, someone might fire him."

"He started at the bottom."
"Yes, and enjoyed it so much he's been there ever since."

"He's such a whinger, if opportunity knocked he'd complain about the noise."

"My brother took an aptitude test to discover what he was best suited for."
"And what did it reveal?"
"That he was best suited for retirement."

"He's the kind of boy girls dream about."
"That's better than seeing him in broad daylight."

"You know how nurses slap babies when they are born?"
"Yes."
"Well, when you were born I reckon they took one look and slapped your mother."

"What do you think of Ada's looks?"
"I don't mind her looking, it's her face I can't stand."

"They say when the photographer took Jim's photo he never developed it."
"Why?"
"He was afraid of being alone with it in a dark room."

"The problem with his face is that his features don't seem to understand the importance of being part of a team."

"Do you think I have a good complexion?"
"Let's just say your face is as smooth as a walnut."

ROSIE: I like being tickled under the chin.
JOSIE: Which one?

MONTY: Does a mud pack help her complexion?
BUNTY: It does for a few days, but then the mud falls off.

118

"Nigel has a Roman nose."
"Yes, it's roamin' here, roamin' there ..."

"His teeth are all his own."
"Has he finished paying for them, then?"

"I think she's quite old, don't you?"
"She's got so many wrinkles on her
forehead she has to screw on her hat."

"Why do you say he's got tennis-match eyes?"
"He's so cross-eyed he can watch both ends of the
court without moving his head."

119

"She's not exactly fat, is she?"
"No, she's got a really faminine look."

"Her sister's skinny, too."
"Yes, when she drinks tomato juice she looks just like a thermometer."

"My girlfriend loves nature."
"That's very good of her, considering what nature has done for her!"

JENNY: Do you like my new suit? I'm told it fits like a glove.
LENNY: Could be – it sticks out in five places.

Hungry Hal was so large he could:
 Take a shower without getting his feet wet.
 Make a room dark by standing in front of the window.
 Fill up the entire back seat of a car.
 Have mumps without anyone realising it.

Beanpole Brenda was so
thin she could:
 Hide behind a telegraph
 pole.
 Disappear when she
 stood sideways.
 Be mistaken for a mop
 when her hair needed
 cutting.
 Hide up a tree even in
 winter.

**WOMAN AT BEDSIDE
OF SICK HUSBAND:**
Doctor, is there any
hope?
DOCTOR: That
depends what you're
hoping for!

DOCTOR: And are you feeling better, Mrs Flabber?

MRS FLABBER: Oh, yes, Doctor, I feel quite my old self again.

DOCTOR: In that case you need more treatment.

MILLY: I've been told I'm out of this world.
WILLY: Many people wish you were!

MANDY: She's a woman of many parts.
ANDY: Pity they were put together so badly.

FIRST BOSS: At least Cynthia's dependable.
SECOND BOSS: Yes, you can depend on her to do the wrong thing.

RYAN: They say she's highly strung.
BRIAN: I always knew she reminded
me of a badly tuned violin.

MOIRA: Your brother's a pig farmer, isn't he?
MAVIS: Yes, how did you know?
MOIRA: He has a certain air about him.

"She's so
poisonous that if
a snake bit her it
would die."

KYLIE: My uncle's just bought a pig.
RILEY: Where will he keep it?
KYLIE: Under the bed.
RILEY: But what about the smell?
KYLIE: The pig will just have to get used to it.

FATHER: Children! How many times must I remind you of your table manners! You're behaving just like pigs!
CHILDREN: That's because our father's an old bore.

"He's so cold-blooded that if a mosquito bit him it would get pneumonia."

"She's so ugly that even spiders run away when they see her."

That's One on You!

LENA: Have you heard the story about the dirty shirt?
LIAM: No.
LENA: That's one on you!

SUSIE: I think a lot of people would go to our teacher's funeral.
SALLY: Yes, to make sure she's dead!

JILL: He makes the most disgusting coffee.
BILL: How do you know?
JILL: A little swallow told me.

HUBERT: I have an answer to everything.
HERBERT: Yes – the wrong one!

HARRIET: She's a boon to the neighborhood. HENRIETTA: Yes, a baboon!

HEAD TEACHER: Teachers like Mr Flopple don't grow on trees, you know.
NEIL (UNDER HIS BREATH): No, they swing from them.

SECRETARY: Did you hear they're going to bury Mr Gromple face down?
COLLEAGUE: No, why's that?
SECRETARY: So he can see where he's going!

"His death won't be listed under 'Obituaries,' it will be under 'Neighborhood Improvements'."

"I hear she's a business woman."
"Yes, her nose is always in other people's business."

"I hear they call him 'Caterpillar.' Why's that?"
"He got where he is by crawling."

"Why's he called 'Rope'?"
"Because he strings people along."

LADY OF THE MANOR: And breakfast is at 7. 30 sharp.
NEW MAID: OK, but if I'm not up you can start without me.

DAVE: They say Don's very courteous.
DUNCAN: Yes, after he's kicked you in the shins he apologizes.

ELLIE: If I'm down in the dumps I buy myself a new dress.
NELLIE: I always wondered where you bought your clothes.

MOTHER: You're pretty dirty, Roger.
ROGER: I'm even prettier clean!

PATTIE: I'd like a dress to match my eyes.
MATTIE: Is it possible to buy a bloodshot dress?

CAMPER: Where do you bathe?
SECOND CAMPER: Oh, I shower in the spring.
CAMPER: I said where, not when.

Two little girls were paddling in the sea on their summer holiday. "Ooh," said one to the other, "your feet aren't half dirty. Didn't you come here last year?"

"When Dave visits the zoo he needs two tickets."
"Why's that?"
"One to get in and one to get out."

"They say he has a waterproof voice."
"What do you mean?"
"It can't be drowned out."

SHEILA: When I go out with John I feel like jumping for joy.
STELLA: Do you? I feel like jumping off a bridge.

"How are you getting on with James?"
"Well, he's a bit dull until you get to know him."
"And when you have got to know him you'll find he's a real bore!"

"He *is* pretty boring."
"Yes, but he has occasional moments of silence."

"He always has to have the last word."
"It wouldn't be so bad if it didn't take him so long to reach it."

TAXI

WIFE: One more word from you and I'm going back to mother!
HUSBAND: Taxi!

HUSBAND: You took me for better or worse.
WIFE: Yes, but I didn't think it would be this much worse.

WIFE: We've been married 12 whole months.
HUSBAND: Seems more like a year to me.

TRACEY: Why aren't you going to marry Dave?
STACEY: Well, he said he'd die if I didn't, so I thought I'd wait and see what happened.

132

SAUL: My wife worships me.
PAUL: Why do you think that?
SAUL: She puts burnt offerings in front of me three times a day.

"They say he's her idol."
"He certainly never does anything."

MYRON: I can marry anyone I please!
BYRON: But you don't please anyone!

"He's very polite, isn't he?"
"Yes, he always takes his shoes off before putting his feet up on the table."

133

WIFE: I've given you the best years of my life.
HUSBAND: Are you asking me for a receipt?

FOREIGN VISITOR: And is this your most charming wife?
HUSBAND: No, she's the only one I've got.

GEMMA: I see more of John than I used to.
EMMA: Yes, he's certainly put on weight.

"She talks so much he's never on speaking terms with her, just listening terms!"

134

"Her chin used to be her best feature – now it's a double feature."

DARREN: I'm afraid I've lost all my money.
SHARON: Oh dear, what a shame. I'll really miss you.

"She's not much of a cook but she can get her husband to boiling point."

"Some husbands can cook, but don't."
"My husband can't cook, but does."

135

"Can your husband cook?"
"Let's just say that yesterday he burnt the salad."

AGGIE: I've made the chicken soup.
MAGGIE: Thank goodness! I thought it was for us!

GUEST: You must have a very clean kitchen.
HOSTESS: How can you tell?
GUEST: All your food tastes of soap.

"She always burns the toast, doesn't she?"
"Yes, her toaster has been declared a fire hazard."

ROBIN: When I was a child my parents almost lost me.
ROBERT: They probably didn't take you far enough into the woods.

MUSICIAN: I play chamber music.
NON-FAN: It sounds more like torture chamber music.

MOTHER: Do you think Sally should take up the piano as a career?
MUSIC TEACHER: No, I think she should put down the lid as a favor.

MOTHER: Julie picked up the piano in no time.
MUSIC TEACHER: Yes, she's certainly a strong girl.

MOTHER: Polly is a natural cello player.
MUSIC TEACHER: You mean she has
bow legs?

"If I were a member of the Noise
Abatement Society I'd send her a
button."
"For her jacket?"
"No, for her lips."

SINGER: Did you like my sad song?
LISTENER: Sad? I'd call it pitiful!

"Her singing's like an old car – it needs a tune-up."

"My sister's singing's an education. Every time she starts I shut myself in my room with my homework."

NORA: This job's driving me mad!
NORMAN: You don't need any driving!

"They're a great trio."
"Yes, three boys with hearts of gold, wills of steel and ears of tin."

"She only cooks health food – you have to be in perfect health in order to eat it and survive."

NEW GARDENER: I was told I should turn my garden over.

EXPERIENCED GARDENER: If I were you I'd turn it over to someone who knows what they're doing!

"There's never a dull moment when Pete's around."

"No, the dullness stretches unbroken for hours!"

"There are a lot of fans at his concerts."

"I expect it's because the management can't run to air conditioning."

"She's a great girl. Everybody loves her!"

"Yes, thousands of fleas can't all be wrong!"

JULIE: I don't know what to buy Grandad for Christmas. He's so rich – what do you buy a man who has everything?
JOHNNY: A watch-dog?

"Why do you call your girlfriend Treasure?"
"Because I wonder where she was dug up!"

WAYNE: John's father taught history, didn't he? He must be quite old now.
JAYNE: Yes, when he was a boy, history was called current affairs.

JENNY: I'm hoping Jerry will give me diamonds for Christmas.
KENNY: Knowing him it's more likely to be spades or clubs!

141

"When he told me he loved me he said he'd go through anything for me."
"And has he?"
"So far he's only gone through my bank account."

"You're like a summer cold!"
"What do you mean?"
"It's impossible to get rid of you!"

"Has success gone to his head?"
"I don't know, but it's certainly gone to his mouth!"

"She's a postman's daughter."
"I thought she knew her males."

"His father's an optician."
"Is that why he makes such a spectacle of himself?"

PATIENT: How can I stop the cold in my head going to my chest?
DOCTOR: Tie a knot in your neck.

"He's like an accordion player."
"What do you mean?"
"He plays both ends against the middle."

JACKIE: I hear John took you to one of the best restaurants in town.
TACKIE: Yes, but he didn't take me in.

"When he was born they fired a 21-gun salute."
"Pity they missed."

"He's so puny, if he ever gets married they won't throw confetti, they'll throw vitamin pills."

"I hear they're planning a runaway wedding."
"Yes, but every time she fixes it up he runs away!"

TARA: I've got a mechanical mind.
TOMMY: Yes, but some of your screws are loose.

SHANE: He has "Ten Commandments" teeth.
WAYNE: What do you mean?
SHANE: They're all broken.

"I've heard he speaks four languages."
"But he can't say 'thank you' in any of them."

"They say he wanted to be a doctor badly."
"Well, he's certainly a bad doctor."

"Why did he want to play the trombone?"
"It's the only instrument on which you can succeed by letting things slide."

"He's so bald you can't look at him in bright sunlight without wearing sunglasses."

ASPIRING ACTRESS: How can I get my name up in lights at the theater?
PRU: Change it to "Exit."

DANIEL: I'll have you know I'm nobody's fool.
DAMIAN: Perhaps we could find someone to adopt you.

CARY: Your face should be painted in oil.
MARY: Why, because I'm beautiful?
CARY: No, because you look like a sardine.

BRYN: I like the simple things in life.
GWYN: Like Tracey?

HARRY: How do you spell "nutcase" with just one letter?
LARRY: I don't know.
HARRY: U.

KERRY: My girlfriend's different from all other girls.
TERRY: I bet she's different. She's the only girl around who'll go out with you!

BOBBIE: You'd make a perfect...
NOBBIE: What?
BOBBIE: Stranger!

What a Cheek!

Knock, knock.
Who's there?
Tom Sawyer.
Tom Sawyer who?
Tom Sawyer bum when you were
changing your pants.

GLYN: You remind me of
a builder's bottom.
WYN: What do you
mean?
GLYN: You're full of bare-
faced cheek!

MOTHER: What did you do to make my little Susie cry,
Simon?
SIMON: I didn't do anything. In fact, I paid her a
compliment.
MOTHER: What did you say?
SIMON: I said she smelled less than any girl I'd ever
known.

LESLEY: Did she really call you a creep?
WESLEY: Yes. She said I was lower than the fluff in an
earthworm's belly button.

LEN: How do you know your grandad's so old?
KEN: He can clean his teeth and whistle at the same time!

JOHN: That girl you went out with was quite pretty.
DON: Yes, if you could read between the lines.

JANE: How often do you go to the dentist?
WAYNE: Twice a year.
JANE: Once for each tooth?

JEAN: Did you know we could get fur from you?
DEAN: Really? What sort?
JEAN: As fur as possible!

PATIENT: Can you cure my fleas?
DOCTOR: Probably. What's wrong with them?

PATTY: What smells worse than a bad egg?
MATTIE: I don't know.
PATTY: You do!

"What do you mean she eats like a bird? She's enormous!"
"I expect she eats worms."

151

GILLY: Do you like my cottage pie?
BILLY: No, it tastes as if you've left the drains in it.

JENNY: Why is your dog giving me such funny looks?
KENNY: You're eating out of his bowl.

DINER: This food isn't fit for a pig!
WAITER: I'll bring you some that is, sir.

SALLY: Sammy's the dirtiest boy I've ever met.
SUSIE: Yes, I've heard his mother cleans out his room with a tractor.

RONNIE: Why are you bathing in such dirty water?
DONNIE: It wasn't dirty when I got in it.

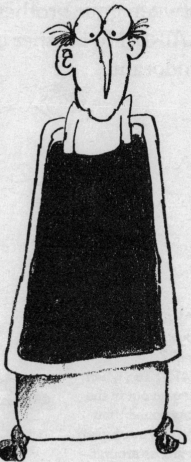

DICK: Why do you smell so peculiar?
RICK: It's soap – I might have known you wouldn't recognize the smell.

JIM: So what happened when you sent your photo to that woman who advertised in the Lonely Hearts column?
KIM: She sent it back saying she wasn't that lonely.

"Did you say she had a sharp tongue?"
"Sharp? I reckon she could carve the Sunday joint with it!"

CLIVE: What's the difference between your brother and a skunk?
CLAIRE: My brother uses a cheaper deodorant.

SARAH: Don't the boys in your class smell?
MARY: Yes, when they go out in the playground they don't so much play as aroma around.

KELLY: Why do you think I should be taller?

SHELLEY: Then you wouldn't be able to smell your feet.

"She's got a figure like school custard."
"How do you mean?"
"Very lumpy!"

What did one cow say to the other?
"You're an udder failure."

"How can I sharpen my appetite?"
"Try eating razor blades."

"You're like an orange – you give me the pip."

"You're like an English bank holiday – wet and depressing."

"You're like a journey to exotic places."
"You mean I'm exciting?"
"No, you make me feel exhausted and ill."

"You're like the *Mona Lisa.*"
"You mean I've got a beautiful smile?"
"No, your face is all dirty and cracked."

156

"I feel run down. What should I take?"
"The number of the car that hit you."

"I feel like a bell."
"Give me a ring next week."

"Why do you say I remind you of a vampire?"
"You have bat breath."

"You smell like Dizzy."
"Dizzy who?"
"Dizzy Nfectant."

I wish I were a little bird
Hiding in a tree.
Then when you passed along below
I'd spatter you with me.

"Do you get on well with your brother?"
"Oh, yes, we stick together."
"Yes, but you don't bath very often, do you?"

NELLY: The wind is getting up.
KELLY: Here, have an indigestion tablet.

MO: Why do you think
the Neverbath rugby
team will win?
JOE: They smell so bad
no one will ever dare
tackle them!

KATE: What was the name of that bungee jumper you used to go out with?

KATH: He was called Ray, but he's X-Ray now.

"You're like an old king."
"What do you mean?"
"You should be throne away."

BILL: I've written you a poem, but you mustn't read it until after my death.

GILL: How wonderful! I can't wait to read it!

HUSBAND: What would you do if I were dead and gone and couldn't pick the strawberries for you?

WIFE: I'd buy frozen ones.

159

ROBERT: You remind me of my nose.
ROBERTA: What do you mean?
ROBERT: You smell.

TRAMP, AT DOOR: Please, Missus,
give us some food.
HOUSEWIFE: Didn't I give you some
home-made meat pie last week?
TRAMP: Yes, but I'm better now.

How can you
keep a very
sweaty man from
smelling?
Cut off his nose!

HENRY: I'd like a pet that I can cuddle.
HENRIETTA: I'll buy you a piranha fish.

BEN: I've just got a new puppy. Would you like to come and see him?
KEN: Does he bite?
BEN: I don't know, that's what I want you to find out.

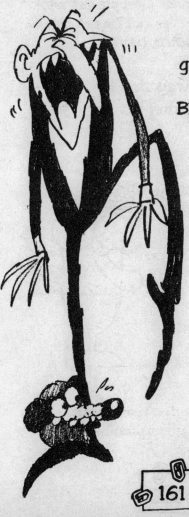

BERT: She certainly gave you a dirty look.
GERT: Who did?
BERT: Mother Nature.

DINER: Waiter, there's a fly in my soup!
WAITER: Don't worry, the spider on your roll will eat it.

MRS SMITH: Is that fishmonger in the High Street any good?
MRS BROWN: He must be – 10,000 flies can't be wrong!

MRS WHITE: Do you miss your husband terribly now he's dead?
MRS BLACK: Yes. I've had so many problems sorting out his estate I sometimes wish he were still alive!

Did you hear about the German boy who pushed his mother off a bridge and said to his friends, "Look, Hans, no Ma!"

PATIENT: Tell me, Doctor, have I got long to live?
DOCTOR: Put it this way, don't start listening to any long-playing records.

MRS SMITH: My Harry has just swallowed a bullet. What shall I do?
DOCTOR: Don't point him at me!

MRS JONES: I'm sorry to call you out so late at night, Doctor.
DOCTOR: That's all right. I had to come out to see old Mr Brown so I thought I might as well kill two birds with one stone.

PATIENT: I'm going to commit suicide.
PSYCHIATRIST: Don't do anything drastic until you've paid my bill.

"I thought I was drowning so I shouted to the lifeguard to throw me something."
"And what did he throw you?"
"A goodbye kiss."

ROMEO: I'd go to the end of the earth for you.
JULIET: Good. And when you get there, jump off!

163

ROMEO: If you won't marry me I'll hang myself from that tree in front of your house.
JULIET: Please don't. You know Father doesn't like young men hanging around in front of the house!

JUDGE: Your first three wives died from eating poisonous mushrooms, and now your fourth wife has drowned in your swimming pool. Isn't that all a bit odd?
PRISONER: Not really. She didn't like mushrooms.

**WIFE: Today we're having Chicken Surprise.
HUSBAND: What's the surprise?
WIFE: You're cooking it.**

When Mr Smith left Mrs Smith, she wrote him a letter, saying, "I missed you this week. Please come home and let me have another shot."

NERVOUS PASSENGER:
How many times do planes
like this crash?
STEWARDESS: Only once!

BARBER: Have you been here before?
CUSTOMER: Yes.
BARBER: I'm afraid I don't remember your face.
CUSTOMER: Well, it's all healed up now.

"But, Mommy, I don't want to go to the Bahamas."
"Shut up and keep swimming."

The teacher was trying to instil into her class the
virtues of hard work. "Take," she said, "the example of
the ant. It works and works all the time. And what is
the result of all this work?"
 Charlie put up his hand.
 "Well, Charlie," said the teacher.
 "Someone treads on it, Miss," he replied.

MOTHER: *Why* did you throw your little sister up in the air?
JIMMY: Well, your friend Mrs Jones said she was a bonny bouncing baby so I just thought I'd check that she bounced.

MOTHER: Stop reaching across the table like that, Samantha. If you want something, ask for it. Haven't you got a tongue in your head?
SAMANTHA: Yes, Mom, but my arm's longer.

LARGE LADY: Could you see me across the street, young man?
CHARLIE: You're so large I could see you across the county!

BRIDEGROOM: Will you really be able to put up with me for the rest of your life?
BRIDE: Of course, dear, you'll be out at work most of the time!

ROMEO:
You
should
have
been
born in
the Dark
Ages.
JULIET:
Why?
ROMEO:
You look
awful in
the light.

A young boy on an airplane was
being a real pain, running up and
down the aisle and shouting.
Finally, one passenger could
stand it no longer. "Hey, kid," he
shouted, "why don't you go and
play outside?"

What were Tarzan's last words?
"Who greased that vine?"

A father who had recently remarried went away on business. When he returned he asked his son how he had got on with his new mother.

"Fine," replied the lad. "Every day she took me across the bay to the island in a boat and left me to swim back."

"Really?" said his father. "Wasn't it hard swimming all that way?"

"A bit," confessed the lad. "But the really hard part was untying the ropes from my legs."

MR GREEN: How did you get on in Australia?
MR BROWN: It was closed.

JEN: You've converted me to religion.
BEN: How do you mean?
JEN: I didn't believe in hell until I met you.

21-gun Salute

"When Johnny was born they fired 21 guns. Trouble was, they all missed."

MIDDLE-AGED HUSBAND: A wife of 40 should be like dollar notes.
HIS FRIEND: How do you mean?
MIDDLE-AGED HUSBAND: You should be able to change her for two of 20.

"I've heard she's fat and ugly."
"I'll say. When she goes to the doctor he tells her to open her mouth and say 'Moo.' "

FIRST MAN: Is your wife fat?
SECOND MAN: Put it this way, when we were married and I carried her across the threshold I had to make two trips.

WOMAN IN BEAUTY PARLOR: What would it take to make me look good?
PROPRIETOR: A fair distance!

A large woman in a flowery hat walked into the church for the wedding.

"Are you a friend of the bride?" asked an usher.

"Certainly not," she snapped. "I'm the groom's mother."

ANGRY VOICE ON PHONE: Is Mr Smith in yet?
DIM SECRETARY: I'm afraid not. He hasn't even been in yesterday yet.

ANOTHER ANGRY VOICE ON THE PHONE: Doesn't your company ever answer letters?
ANOTHER DIM SECRETARY: Oh dear, haven't you got our letter, yet? I'm about to post it to you.

BOSS: That new clerk is useless.
PERSONNEL MANAGER: Oh dear.
BOSS: Yes, he's only been here a week and already he's a month behind in his work!

BOSS: Why do you want two weeks off work to get married? You've just had some time off, why didn't you get married then?
SECRETARY: I didn't want to spoil my holiday.

TEACHER: What's the difference between the death rate in Elizabethan times and the death rate nowadays?
SMART SUE: It's the same, Miss – one death per person.

POLICE OFFICER: Have you ever been shoplifting?
SUSPECT: That's my business!
POLICE OFFICER: Oh, you're a professional, are you?

ROMEO: Will you come to the cinema with me tonight?
JULIET: Oh, no, I never go out with perfect strangers.
ROMEO: Who says I'm perfect?

JULIET: Whisper those three little words that will make my day.
ROMEO: Go to hell!

"They say she's been asked to get married hundreds of times."
"Really? Who by?"
"Her parents!"

"If we get married do you think you'll be able to live on my income?"
"Of course. But what will you live on?"

"She's been married to so many rich men and then divorced she must have got richer by decrees."

WAITER, TO MAN WHO'S BEEN SITTING WAITING FOR 50 MINUTES: Will you have some food, sir?
MAN: No thanks, I don't want to waste my lunch hour.

"Is it possible to tell when a politician is lying?"
"Oh yes, I can always tell."
"How?"
"Their lips move."

JENNY: How can I make my money go further?
LENNY: Post it abroad.

"Why do you say your granny is stupid?"
"Because when she reads the obituary columns she always asks why people die in alphabetical order."

"Why do you say your uncle is spiteful?"
"Because when the doctor said he had rabies he immediately wrote a list of people he wanted to bite."

"You can always spot my wife at a party."
"How?"
"Look for two people talking. If one of them looks bored, the other is my wife."

"Is he a self-made man?"
"Oh, yes. And he's devoted to his maker."

"They say he's hated so much even his own shadow refuses to follow him about."

SUSIE: Do you think I'm looking good?
SIMON: You've never looked better in your life – whenever *that* was.

DAVE: Is your sister beautiful?
DON: Well, if she were a building I'd say she'd be condemned.

CLARA: Is that open-air theater in the park bad, then?
CLARENCE: It's so bad that at last night's performance six trees walked out.

GILLIE: Did the bride look beautiful?
MILLIE: She wore a lovely dress. I wonder when that style will be in fashion again?

Two actors were talking about a glamorous young starlet. "I like her dresses," said the first.

"Yes," replied the second. "They certainly seem to bring out the bust in her."

"That singer only got to the top because her dresses didn't."

MRS SMITH: My husband has a good head for money.
MRS JONES: Do you mean it's got a little slot in the top?

177

HARRY: Is your girlfriend conceited?
LARRY: I think so. She only looks at me so she can see her reflection in my glasses.

MAISIE: Is your boyfriend fat?
DAISY: No, he's just a meter or so too short for his body.

"When he was a baby he was so ugly his parents ran away from home."

MR BLACK: I took my wife to the beauty parlor yesterday and had to sit and wait all afternoon for her.
MR WHITE: Whatever was she having done?
MR BLACK: Nothing – she just went for an estimate.

178

"Did you hear that Harry had
gone to medical school?"
"No, what's he studying?"
"Nothing, they're studying him."

MRS BROWN: I took my
son to the zoo yesterday.
MRS GREEN: Did they
accept him?

MRS MUGFACE: How your little
daughter's grown!
MRS JUGFACE: Yes, she's certainly
gruesome.

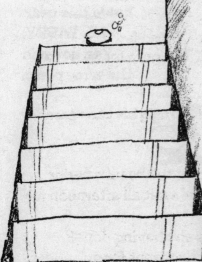

Mrs Moan was complaining
about her husband. "I'm
getting really fed up with
him," she said. "What shall
I do?"
"You could try the soft
soap treatment," replied
her friend, Mrs Groan.
"I did," said Mrs Moan.
"But he spotted it at the
top of the stairs."

Millie and Tilly were discussing a friend who was a pickpocket. "Does she pick the pockets of strangers?" asked Millie.

"Only those she doesn't know," replied Tilly.

"I have a dual personality."
"As what I have to say to you is strictly confidential, one of you had better wait outside."

"Your socks are full of holes."
"I don't give a darn."

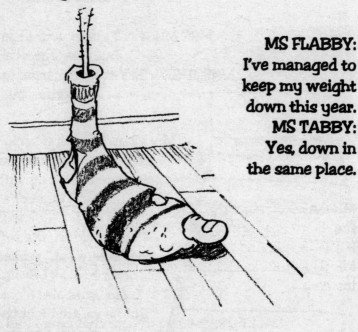

MS FLABBY:
I've managed to keep my weight down this year.
MS TABBY:
Yes, down in the same place.

PATIENT: My hair seems to be getting thinner.
DOCTOR: Why do you want fat hair?

HARRY: I think I've got an inferiority complex.
LARRY: Rubbish! You *are* inferior!

MR GARGLE: My wife thought she was a crocodile and the doctor said she should be locked away.
MR GURGLE: And was she?
MR GARGLE: No, I had her made into a pair of shoes instead.

SALLY: I was sorry to hear that your head teacher died. What was the complaint?
DARREN: There haven't been any yet.

DOCTOR: How are you, Mr Grumble?
MR GRUMBLE: I'm having problems with my
breathing, Doctor.
DOCTOR: Oh, we can soon put a stop to that.

DOCTOR: I can't find anything wrong
with you. It must be the drink.
PATIENT: OK, I'll come back when
you're sober.

SURGEON: I think you've just cut an artery.
MEDICAL STUDENT: Oh, dear, aorta know better.

FAT LADY: I'd love to be able to diet, but
I've no willpower.
THIN LADY: You're just a wishful shrinker.

ANOTHER FAT LADY: What's the best way to slim?
ANOTHER THIN LADY: Don't exceed the feed limit.

182

A doctor was searching in one of the hospital's flower beds when a passerby asked if he had lost something.

"No," he replied. "It's just that we have to do a heart transplant on a head teacher, and I was looking for a stone of the right size."

The school pupils were being given vaccinations, and when it was Jimmy's turn he asked for the sticking plaster to be put on his other arm.

"But if I put it on the arm that's had the vaccination your friends will know not to bump into it," said the nurse.

Jimmy replied, "You don't know my friends."

PATIENT: Are you sure I'll get better, Doctor? I heard of a doctor who was treating someone for appendicitis and they died of stomach cancer.
DOCTOR: Don't worry, when I treat someone for appendicitis they die of appendicitis.

WIFE: The hospital can't do my operation yet, there isn't a bed available.
HUSBAND: Oh dear. That means you'll have to go on talking about your previous operation for a bit longer.

BOSS: You're looking much better now, Reynolds. How's that pain?
REYNOLDS: She's away on a business trip.

"I think I'm a bit overweight."
"Nonsense! Pull up three chairs and we'll talk about it."

JOHNNY: What's the difference between you and a book?
RONNIE: I don't know.
JOHNNY: You can shut up a book.

184

"How can I cure water on the knee?"
"Wear pumps."

SANDY: Do you like the cinema?
MANDY: The trouble with most films is that they shoot too much film and not enough actors.

NELLIE: Is your auntie old?
KELLY: Old? When she was born Billy wasn't even a kid!

MICKEY: Why do you say I'm like blotting paper?
DICKEY: You soak everything up but you get it all backwards.

185

"They say his violin playing is improving. People only put earplugs in one ear now."

"His teeth stick out so much I thought his nose was playing a piano."

GORDON: I think I've got a sixth sense.
JORDAN: You must have, because there's no sign of the other five.

PADDY: Would you say the kids at your school are tough?
MADDIE: Tough? Even the teachers play truant!

UNDER 5's

LIZZIE: Listening to you is like hearing a dripping tap.
DIZZIE: How do you mean?
LIZZIE: You can always hear it but you can't turn it off.

DON: Is your Dad bald?
RON: His head's like a parting with ears.

"She talks so much she's the only person I know who has to rub suntan lotion into her tongue."

"Are they happily married?"
"Oh, yes. She's happy and he's married."

"Why do you say my voice is like a pirate?"
"It's murder on the high Cs."

"Why do you call me your melancholy baby?"
"You've got a figure like a melon and a face like a collie."

"Your beard looks as if it goes to the same vet as my dog."

"Mean? If he were a ghost he wouldn't even give you a fright."

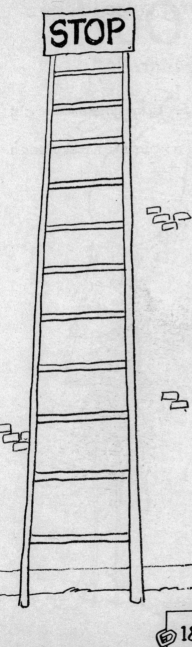

"He's got the kind of face I don't want to remember but find very difficult to forget."

"That builder's so stupid he's got a notice saying 'Stop' on the top of his ladder."

"Why did you give up your work at the bakery?"
"It was a crummy job."

"I've heard you believe in the hereafter."
"That's right."
"Then hereafter leave me alone!"

Watch Out!

What's the difference between a wild camel and a bully?
One's a big, smelly, bad-tempered beast and the other is an animal.

Why are bullies like bananas?
Because they're yellow and hang around in bunches.

"Simon's a bully and thinks he's really hard."
"He will be when we've poured this concrete over him."

"You're very ugly."
"Yes, and you're quite good-looking – for a gorilla, that is."

"You remind me of a toenail."
"What do you mean?"
"The sooner you're cut down to size the better."

"You remind me of a calendar."
"How do you mean?"
"Your days are numbered."

SHANE: I'm a big noise round here.
JANE: You shouldn't eat so many baked beans then.

"He'll never make a photographer."
"Why not?"
"Every time he's in a dark room trouble develops."

DARREN: My report says I'm hopeless at lessons –
lazy, dirty, unpunctual, and that I fight with other
children.
SHARON: I'm pleased you've improved since last term.

JIMMY: Go and squirt lemon juice in your eyes.
TIMMY: What for?
JIMMY: It's the only way to make you smart.

"You're like an oil well."
"What do you mean?"
"Always boring."

JENNY: Go and sit down.
KENNY: Why?
JENNY: Cos nobody can
stand you.

JAMES: Do you know what nice people do at the weekend?
JOHN: No.
JAMES: I didn't think you would.

SUE: You'd make a good exchange student.
PRU: Do you think so?
SUE: Yes. We might be able to exchange you for someone nice.

SIMON: You remind me of a camel.
SHEILA: Why?
SIMON: You give me the hump.

Why did the thug have lumps of earth sewn on to his clothes? Because his name was mud.

Mervyn showed his friends a
picture taken at the seaside
when he was having a donkey
ride on the beach. "This is me
on holiday," he said.
"Very nice," said
his friend Martin.
"But who's that on
your back?"

"I've been told I have the face of a saint."
"Yes, a Saint Bernard."

DAVE: You should swallow a magnet.
MAVE: Why?
DAVE: It's the only way you'll make yourself more
attractive.

"She should have been born in the Dark Ages."
"You mean she is old-fashioned?"
"No, just that she looks terrible in the light."

"Why do you call her 'Amazon'? Is it because she's big and strong?"
"No, it's because she's wet and wide."

"I'll have you know I'm not stupid, my brain is in perfect condition."
"That's true, it's never been used."

"Look here, what I say goes!"
"Say your name then!"

JOHN: When I grow up I'm going to have letters after my name.
DON: Such as S T U P I D?

KATE: I always speak my mind.
KATH: I'm surprised you've so much to say, then.

JUDE: Your parents aren't from this country, are they?
JADE: No, but at least they're from this planet.

What's the difference between a bully and gravy? Gravy's only thick some of the time.

JEMIMA: Remember I'm a big name in these parts.
JONATHAN: Yes, THICK AND STUPID is quite a mouthful.

KEITH: I'm looking for a job. What shall I do?

KEVIN: Apply at the cobbler's, I've heard he's looking for heels.

GEORGE: I'm not waiting in this queue, I'm going in front of you!

GRAHAM: Good, it means I won't have to look at your face.

BRIAN: I do what I like.

BRENDA: You mean you like acting like an idiot?

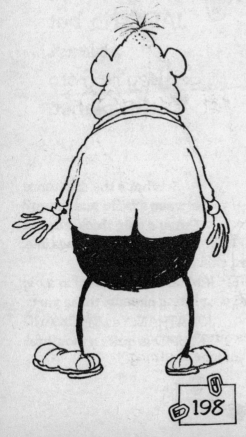

"You're like a remote control."

"How do you mean?"

"You turn everybody off."

198

LEN: Can I come fishing with you?
BEN: No, I've got enough maggots already.

KEVIN: Hey, man, the girls think I'm cool.
KIERAN: Me too – as cool as a cod.
KEVIN: Why a cod?
KIERAN: I've always thought you were a real cold fish.

FATHER: Young Andy picks things up very well.
MOTHER: You don't mean he's started shoplifting already?

"She's a person of rare gifts."
"Yes, she never gives anyone anything."

199

"He's a person of rare intelligence."
"Yes, he hasn't got much."

NEDDY: I've got a cold in the head.
TEDDY: It must be the first time you've had anything in your head.

"Gemma's like a rare flower."
"You mean she's beautiful?"
"No, everyone wants to know where she was dug up."

WILL: What's the difference between you and Robin Hood?
BILL: I don't know.
WILL: Robin was a big hero, you're a big zero.

JIM: What's dirty and smelly and found in your underwear?
TIM: I don't know.
JIM: You!

"Success hasn't changed her."
"No, she's just as awful as she always was."

"Let's just say he's got a hat full of cement."
"What do you mean?"
"He's a blockhead."

"You remind me of a kettle."
"Why?"
"You get everyone steamed up!"

CLARENCE: I intend to go far in life.
CLARA: The sooner, and the further, the better!

JULIE: I was a big hit in the school choir.
JANEY: With rotten eggs?

MIKE: You'd make a good baker.
SPIKE: Why?
MIKE: You're very good at loafing around.

PEGGY: I'm going to thump Fred. He told me I was stupid.
PETER: Don't take any notice of him. He's only repeating what everyone else says.

BERT: Are you an elastic band?
GERT: No. Why?
BERT: Then stop snapping at people.

BILL: Are you a clock?
BEN: No. Why?
BILL: You keep winding me up.

MARY: Everyone says I've got a big mouth. What should I do?
GARY: Buy a bigger toothbrush?

CHARLIE: I'd like to talk to you in kangaroo-speak.
CLARE: What would you say?
CHARLIE: Hop it!

HEAVY: This place isn't big enough for the two of us.
HARVEY: You'd better go on a diet, then!

DAVE: What did your teacher say when you took your pet bulldog to school?
DON: He said, "You can't bring that ugly brute in here."
DAVE: What happened then?
DON: The bulldog said, "It's not my fault, *he* brought *me*."

"Do you know what we'd get if we crossed you with a bottom?"
"What?"
"A no-good bum."

"You'd make a good model."
"Because of my looks?"
"No, because you're such a poser."

CLARA: I'm so bright I'm going to cut down my studying time by half.
SARAH: Which half are you going to cut out – thinking about studying or talking about studying?

"He told me I would sleep like a log."
"And then what?"
"He put my bed in the fireplace."

TILLY: Do you have any sisters or brothers?
MILLY: No, I'm an only child.
TILLY: Thank goodness for that!

LOUISE: What's the difference between you and a baby lamb?
LIONEL: I don't know.
LOUISE: The lamb will one day be a sheep, but you'll always be a creep.

STELLA: You only have one use in life.
ELLA: What's that?
STELLA: Your face can cure hiccups!

ANNE: Where
are you in the
class photo?
DAN
(POINTING):
There.
ANNE: Oh, I
didn't
recognize you
with your
mouth shut.

MERYL: There's no point in
arguing. We just have to face
the fact that we've got opposite
personalities.
CHERYL: What do you mean?
MERYL: I've got personality,
you have the opposite.

PAT: I only sing in the bath.
WAT (SNIFFING): You obviously don't sing very often!

WALLY: If frozen water is
       iced water, what is
       frozen ink?
SALLY: Iced ink.
WALLY: I know
       you do!

"I told him words can hurt, but he disagreed."
"Did you prove your point?"
"Oh, yes, I threw the encyclopedia at him."

"When you're with him you need a long neck."
"Why?"
"Because then your nose is further away from his feet!"

JOHN: I'd hate to be in your shoes.
CON: And *I'd* hate to be in yours – I know what your feet smell like!

ANDY: My dad's stronger than your dad.
MANDY: He must be after raising a dumb-bell like you!

Adding
Insult to
Injury

WILLIAM: Bill's so suspicious, isn't he?
WILFRED: Yes. Even his eyes watch each other all the time.

PETER: Did you hear about the idiot who goes around saying "No" all the time?
ANITA: No.
PETER: So it's you, is it?

STAN: You remind me of the sea.
SUE: Because I'm so wild and romantic?
STAN: No, because you make me sick!

ALISON: You argue so much you're
like a skunk.
ALBERT: A skunk?
ALISON: Yes, you raise such a stink!

JIM: People keep throwing
me in the dustbin.
TIM: Don't talk rubbish!

What do you say to
someone who keeps bees?
"Buzz off!"

What do you say to someone
with a wooden leg?
"Hop it!"

What do you say to someone who can't sleep?
"Lie at the edge of the bed, you'll soon drop
off."

What do you say to someone who fits doors?
"Don't fly off the handle."

What do you
say to someone
who fits
windows?
"Go away,
you're a real
pane."

ADA: I've only got a
few seconds to live.
AMY: Can you just
wait a minute?

What do you say to
someone with flat feet?
"Would you like to borrow
my bicycle pump?"

CHLOE: I need something for my liver.
ZOE: Here's a pound of onions.

BETH: I think I've got water on the brain.
SETH: You need a tap on the head.

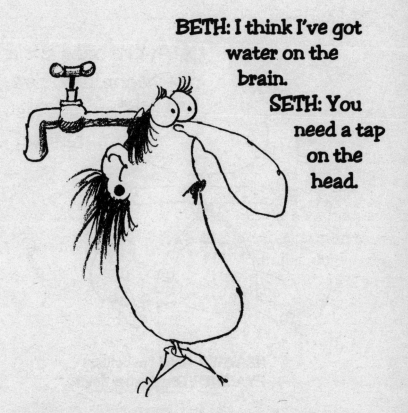

LEE: I snore so loudly I wake myself up.
LIZ: Try sleeping in the next room.

MRS EVANS: Help! The baby's swallowed my pen! What shall I do?
MRS JONES: Use a pencil.

HEATHER: Help! I'm boiling!
HYACINTH: Oh, simmer down.

CECIL: I've just swallowed a whole lot of pool balls.
COLIN: What color were they?
CECIL: Brown, pink and red.
COLIN: Eat some greens and you'll be all right.

ERROL: I feel so run down.
ERNIE: You should look both ways before you cross the street.

JERRY: I feel like a strawberry.
TERRY: You *are* in a jam, aren't you?

EUSTACE: I feel like an onion.
ESMOND: You *are* in a pickle.

DAISY: I think there's something wrong with my stomach.
MAISY: If you keep your coat fastened I don't suppose anyone will notice.

GEOFF: What can I do about wind?
GEORGE: You can borrow my kite if you like.

STEWART: I keep thinking I'm invisible.
STEVE: Who said that?

I KEEP THINKING I'M INVISIBLE.

CELIA: The food at our school is terrible.
AMELIA: Yes, even the dustbins get indigestion.

MRS FEATHER: I'm off to get my hair done.
MR FEATHER: Going to the ugly parlor again, are you?

"They say he's a millionaire and lives in a twenty-room mansion, but he always looks grubby and doesn't smell too good."
"I guess he's just *filthy rich*."

JOE: I know a café where we can eat dirt cheap.
FLO: I don't want to eat dirt.
JOE: I thought that was what you lived on.

MOTHER: What did you say when Aunty Lucy gave you an apple?
LITTLE LULU: Peel it.

JAMIE: Is your new girlfriend good-looking?
HAMISH: Yes, except for her pedestrian eyes.
JAMIE: What are pedestrian eyes?
HAMISH: They look both ways before they cross.

KAREN: You know, I saved up for years to buy that wonderful German car.
SHARON: Did you get it?
KAREN: Yes. And the first time I took it out someone drove into the back of it.
SHARON: I guess that's the way the Mercedes Benz.

JANE: Now we're engaged I hope you'll give me a ring.
SHANE: Of course I will. What's your phone number?

"I wouldn't say he's dishonest,
but if he eats in a restaurant he
thinks of the cutlery as being a
kind of medicine."
"How do you mean?"
"To be taken after meals."

MRS SMITH: What were you before you
came to teach at this school?
MRS JONES: Happy.

MOTHER: Why is your little sister crying?
JIMMY: Because I won't give her my
sandwich.
MOTHER: What about her own sandwich?
JIMMY: She cried when I ate that too.

JACK: I was chosen by a computer as being an ideal boyfriend.
JOHN: A computer's about the only thing that would have *you* as a boyfriend!

DICK: I got a lovely puppy for my girlfriend.
MICK: I wish I could make a swap like that.

KATIE: Are you still looking for a husband?
KATHY: Yes.
KATIE: What's the problem?
KATHY: I can't find anyone clever enough to make a lot of money and daft enough to spend it all on me.

MAISIE: My boyfriend's really intelligent. They say he has brains enough for two.
DAISY: He sounds like the right man for you, then.

"Why do they call her an after-dinner speaker?"
"Because every time she speaks to a man she's after a dinner."

GUY: What did you buy your girlfriend for her birthday?
CY: I got her a bottle of toilet water. It was very expensive.
GUY: You should have come round to our house. The water in our toilet is free.

223

"They say he fell in love with his wife the second time he met her. The first time he didn't know how rich she was."

YOUNG MAN: I've come to ask for your daughter's hand.
FATHER: You'll have to take the rest of her too.

SHONA: My boyfriend says I'm beautiful.
RONA: They do say love is blind.

GARY: My new girlfriend's a crazy chick.
CARY: She must be to go out with a worm like you.

TOM: Could you be happy
with a boy like me?
TRISH: Maybe, if you weren't
around too often.

MRS ROSE: Where are you going to?
MRS THORN: The doctor's. I don't like the
look of my husband.
MRS ROSE: Can I come with you? I can't
stand the sight of mine!

HOLLY: How are you getting on with your
advertisements for a husband? Have you had any
replies?
MOLLY: Yes, lots. And they all say the same – take
mine!

225

SHARON: Do you like me?
DARREN: As girls go, you're fine. And the further you go, the better.

CLARK: I'm not rich like Arwin, and I don't have a country estate like Brian or a Ferrari like Clive, but I love you and I want to marry you.
CLARA: I love you too, but what did you say about Brian?

BRIAN: Why are you covered with scratches?
BYRON: My girlfriend said it with flowers.
BRIAN: That sounds romantic.
BYRON: It wasn't, she hit me round the head with a bunch of roses.

JUDY: I wish I had a cent for every boy who's asked me out.
TRUDY: Then you'd be able to afford to use a public toilet.

SAMANTHA: Do you really love me?
SIMON: Oh yes.
SAMANTHA: Then whisper something soft and sweet in my ear.
SIMON: Lemon meringue pie.

"My wife thinks she's a door."
"Let me know when she's unhinged."

"My husband thinks he's a squirrel."
"I expect he's just another nut-case."

POLLY: If you were my husband I'd put poison in your tea.
SOLLY: And if I were your husband I'd drink it.

MRS BRIGGS: Wake up! There's a burglar in the kitchen eating my meat pies!
MR BRIGGS: Who shall I call, the police or an ambulance?

MR HEDGE: I say, old boy, you just shot my wife!
MR TREE: So sorry, old lad, have a shot at mine!

TILLY: Who's that woman with the little wart?
MILLY: Shh, he's her husband.

PETER: That man is the ugliest person I've ever seen!
ANITA: He's my husband.
PETER: Oh dear, I'm so sorry.
ANITA: *You're* sorry.

MR LONG:
My wife's one in a million.
MS SHORT:
Really? I thought she was won in a raffle!

"They're a perfect couple – he works in a chip shop and there's something fishy about her."

"I wouldn't say he was dishonest, but if he worked in an orchestra he'd be one of the fiddlers."

Getting Even

FREDA: Do you like my new hairstyle?
FREDDIE: It's brilliant. It covers most of your face.

JOHNNY: What's the matter with Jim?
DONNY: I think he's got hereditary diarrhea.
JOHNNY: What's hereditary diarrhea?
DONNY: It runs in the genes.

BRENDA: My dad says intelligence reigns supreme in our family.
GLENDA: Obviously it didn't rain the day you were born.

232

HAZEL: I wouldn't say you were stupid . . .
HEATHER: Oh good.
HAZEL: . . . but if you have an idea in your head it's in solitary confinement.

JERRY: I could be a famous brain surgeon if I had a mind to.
TERRY: Yes, that's the problem, isn't it? You don't have a mind.

LOUISE: Did you hear about the stupid hitchhiker?
LIZA: No, what did he do?
LOUISE: He started his journey early so there wouldn't be so much traffic about.

Knock, knock.
Who's there?
Honda.
Honda who?
Honda stand what I'm
talking about?

Knock, knock.
Who's there?
Datsun.
Datsun who?
Datsun other lousy
joke!

Knock, knock.
Who's there?
One-eye.
One-eye who?
You're the
One-eye
can't
stand!

234

Knock, knock.
Who's there?
Punch.
Punch who?
Punch you on the nose
if you don't shut up!

Knock, knock.
Who's there?
Doughnut.
Doughnut who?
Doughnut come near
me, I can't stand you!

Knock, knock.
Who's there?
R.U.
R.U. who?
R.U. really as stupid
as you seem?

Knock, knock.
Who's there?
Ammonia.
Ammonia who?
Ammonia going to tell
you once – go away!

MYRA: You're like a non-slip rug.
MYRON: How do you mean?
MYRA: Covered in pimples.

"They're very well matched. She's blinded
by love and his looks are out of sight."

"My beauty is timeless."
"Well, yes, your face could certainly stop a clock."

TAMMY: Did you like my curry?
SAMMY: Did you buy it yourself?

MOTHER: Go and wash your face. I can see what you had for lunch.
DENNIS: What was it?
MOTHER: Meat and gravy – I can still see the gravy.
DENNIS: You're wrong. It was fish – the meat and gravy were yesterday.

BOSS: Why did you sack your secretary?
COLLEAGUE: Sickness.
BOSS: You mean you sacked her because she was ill?
COLLEAGUE: No, because the sight of her made me sick.

MRS BEETLE: What do you want for Christmas?
MR BEETLE: I'd like an electrical gadget.
MRS BEETLE: How about an electric chair?

HOTEL PORTER: May I carry your bag, sir?
HOTEL GUEST: That won't be necessary, my wife is perfectly capable of walking.

ALANA: I see you're an expert on Ancient Greece.
ALAN: What do you mean?
ALANA: You never wash your hair.

"I wouldn't say you were clumsy, but if you fell over you'd miss the floor!"

"Waiter! There's a film on my soup!"
"Then why don't you shut up and watch it?"

"Waiter! Why is there a button in my potato?"
"It's a jacket potato, idiot."

"I wouldn't say he was lazy but he sticks his nose out of the window for the wind to blow it for him."

"What do you mean I'm temperamental?"
"Half bad-tempered and half mental!"

MOTHER: If you eat your greens you'll grow up to be a beautiful young woman.
MILLY: Why didn't you eat your greens when you were young?

JIMMY: We've got the right dinner for an idiot like you.
TIMMY: What's that?
JIMMY: Chump chops.

BILLY: Since I met you I haven't been able to eat or drink.
TILLY: Because you love me so much?
BILLY: No, because I'm broke.

JERRY: You remind me of a biscuit.
TERRY: A lovely chocolate one?
JERRY: No, a gingernut, you red-headed loony.

240

GRANDMA: Did you enjoy my stew?

GILLIE: No, not really. It wasn't very good.

GRANDMA: I've been making stews since before you were born.

GILLIE: Why did you have to save one for me?

EDWARD: Tell me you love me or I'll hang myself from the tree in your garden.

EDWINA: Please don't, I hate people hanging around outside.

BARBARA: Bernie has a heart of gold.

BRENDA: You mean he's kind and good-natured?

BARBARA: No, he's hard and yellow.

DAVE: What makes you think your mother
hates you?
MAVE: Why else would she pack a road map
with my lunch?

DARREN: I'm so thirsty my
tongue's hanging out.
SHARON: Is that your tongue? I
thought it was a horrible spotted
tie!

CLARA: Every time
Claud sits next to
me at meals he eats
his head off.
SARAH: Yes, but he
looks better that
way, don't you
think?

NINA: They're a good partnership.
TINA: Yes, she goes jogging and he's on the run
from the law.

NIGEL: Have you noticed how many girls
don't want to get married nowadays?
NEIL: No. How do you know?
NIGEL: I've asked them all.

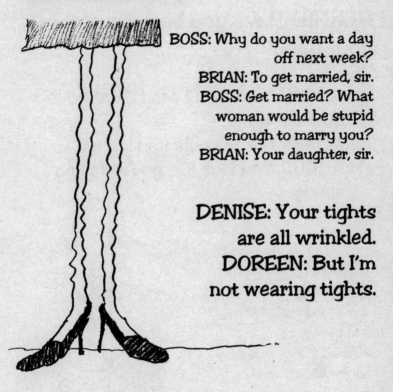

BOSS: Why do you want a day
off next week?
BRIAN: To get married, sir.
BOSS: Get married? What
woman would be stupid
enough to marry you?
BRIAN: Your daughter, sir.

DENISE: Your tights
are all wrinkled.
DOREEN: But I'm
not wearing tights.

NORBERT: You remind me of a pie.
NOREEN: Really? Am I sweet?
NORBERT: No, but you've got some crust.

BERNIE: What's the matter with your finger?
ERNIE: I think I've got a splinter in it.
BERNIE: Have you been scratching your head?

ANGUS: Have you been talking to yourself again?
ADAM: Yes, how did you know?
ANGUS: You look like you're falling asleep.

Knock, knock.
Who's there?
Stan.
Stan who?
Stan back, his breath smells awful!

Knock, knock.
Who's there?
Juliet.
Juliet who?
Juliet so much
she burst!

Knock, knock.
Who's there?
Cyril.
Cyril who?
Cyril pleasure when
you leave!

Knock, knock.
Who's there?
Anita.
Anita who?
Anita you like I need a
black eye!

Knock, knock.
Who's there?
Toyota.
Toyota who?
Toyota be a law against
people like you.

Knock, knock.
Who's there?
Datsun.
Datsun who?
Datsun awful dress
you're wearing!

Knock, knock.
Who's there?
Sarah.
Sarah who?
Sarah any way to
get you out of my
life?

Knock, knock.
Who's there?
Joe-jum.
Joe-jum who?
Joe-jum poff a cliff!

Knock, knock.
Who's there?
Joan.
Joan who?
Joan call us, we'll call you!

246

CHILDREN'S BOOKS AVAILABLE FROM ROBINSON PUBLISHING

The Biggest Joke Book in the World   *Tom & Matt Keegan*   *£6.99*
All the jokes you will ever need to know.

The Ultimate Book of Wisecracks and Insults
   Sandy Ransford   *£3.99*
Insults and comebacks for every occasion. Never again be at a loss for a funny reply.

The Joke Museum
   Sandy Ransford   *£3.99*
A collection of the finest, funniest and oldest jokes in the world.

The A–Z Encyclopedia of Jokes
   £6.99
A giant selection of jokes about every subject you can think of, from A to Z.

1001 Knock Knock Jokes
   Jasmine Birtles   *£3.99*
All the old favorites and some hilarious new ones.

The Ultimate Book of Unforgettable Creepy Crawly Jokes
   Liz Hughes   *£6.99*
Jokes about everything from slugs and mosquitoes, bees and bats to creepy ghouls and witches' cats.

1001 Animal Quacker Jokes   *Jasmine Birtles*   *£3.99*
There are jokes in here for every animal you can imagine . . . and some you can't!

The Biggest Book of Stupid Jokes in the Universe   *David Mostyn*   *£6.99*
Jam-packed with a spectacular selection of the most incredibly stupid – but hilariously funny – jokes.

Big Bad Classroom Jokes   *Sandy Ransford*   *£3.99*
All the very best jokes to be invented in the classroom.

The Biggest Book of Mazes in the World *£5.99*
Amazing collection of baffling mazes – prepare for hours of bafflement,
backtracking and bumblings as you try to reach the end!

The Puzzle Factory   *Sue Preston* *£3.99*
The ultimate puzzle challenge, to keep even the brightest minds occupied for
hours.

The Biggest Book of Puzzles in the World *£5.99*
Nutty word games, mad mazes, codes to crack and hundreds more puzzle
challenges.

Dance Stories   *Felicity Trotman* *£4.99*
Wonderful collection of exciting, glamorous and romantic stories about the world
of dance.

Fantasy Stories   *Mike Ashley* *£4.99*
Some of the best fantasy stories of the century. Many have been written especially
for this book, others are classics.

Robinson books are available from all good bookshops or can be ordered direct
from the publisher. Just tick the title you want and fill in the form below.

Robinson Publishing Ltd, PO Box 11, Falmouth, Cornwall TR10 9EN
Tel: +44(0) 1326 374900 Fax: +44(0) 1326 374888 Email: books@Barni.avel.co.uk

UK/BFPO customers please allow £1.00 for p&p for the first book, plus 50p for the second,
plus 30p for each additional book up to a maximum charge of £3.

Overseas customers (inc. Ireland) please allow £2.00 for the first book, plus £1.00 for the
second, plus 50p for each additional book.

Please send me the titles ticked above.

NAME (Block letters) ....

ADDRESS ....

....POSTCODE ....

I enclose a cheque/PO (payable to Robinson Publishing Ltd) for ....
I wish to pay by Switch/Credit Card

....Card Expiry Date ....